# The Safe, Self-Confident Child

SIGNAL HILL™
PUBLICATIONS

This book was produced in
collaboration with
**MELD.**

1997 printing; ISBN 1-56853-037-4
Copyright © 1994
Signal Hill Publications

An imprint of New Readers Press
U.S. Publishing Division of Laubach Literacy International
Box 131, Syracuse, New York 13210-0131

All rights reserved. No part of this book may be reproduced or transmitted in any form or by any means, electronic or mechanical, including photocopying, recording, or by any information storage and retrieval system, without permission in writing from the publisher.
Printed in the United States of America

Information graphics by Shane Kelley
Illustrations by Richard Ewing
Cover photo: BORLAND STOCK PHOTO
Cover design: Kimbrly Koennecke

9 8 7 6 5 4 3 2

Library of Congress Cataloging-in-Publication Data

The safe, self-confident child.
  p. cm. — (For your information)
"This book was produced in collaboration with
MELD"—Copyright page.
ISBN 1-56420-033-7
 1. Safety education.  2. Children's accidents—Prevention.
 3. Child rearing.  4. Readers (Adult)
 I. Series: For your information (Syracuse, N.Y.)
HQ770.7.S24    1994
649'.1—dc20                                       93-40577
                                                     CIP

# Contents

Preface .................................................. 5

Raising a Child ..................................... 7

## Part 1  The Safe Child

**Chapter 1**
Preventing Accidents ...................... 10

**Chapter 2**
Making Your Home Safe .............. 20

**Chapter 3**
Preventing Illness ............................ 24

## Part 2  The Self-Confident Child

**Chapter 4**
The Right Attitude ......................... 30

**Chapter 5**
Guidance ........................................... 34

**Chapter 6**
How Are You Doing? ..................... 47

## Part 3  Special Ages, Special Needs

Chapter 7
Babies .................................................................. 52

Chapter 8
Toddlers (Ages 1–3) ......................................... 57

Chapter 9
Preschoolers (Ages 4–5) ................................. 70

Chapter 10
Older Kids (Ages 6–9) ..................................... 75

Chapter 11
Preteens (Ages 9–12) ...................................... 86

Chapter 12
Teenagers (Ages 13 and Up) ......................... 91

## Part 4  Resources

Where to Get Help ........................................... 94

# Preface

Information is power.

Being informed means being able to make choices. When you can make choices, you are not helpless. Having information is the first step toward being in control of a situation. It is a way to get more out of life.

This book, *The Safe, Self-Confident Child*, discusses issues that affect anyone who is raising a child. It gives useful information and ideas for raising children to be independent.

This book was developed with help from MELD. MELD is a program for parents of young children. MELD programs and materials are used by parents of different ages and from different cultures. MELD groups meet in more than 70 communities around the country. You can reach MELD at (612) 332-7563.

Thanks to the following people for their contribution to the content of *The Safe, Self-Confident Child:* Ann Ellwood, former Executive Director of MELD; Mary Nelson, Publications Director of MELD; and Ann Walker Smalley, writing consultant to MELD.

Special thanks to Carol J. Moore for her writing and expertise, and to Vivek Apte for his research and content contributions.

## In this book

- *Parent* means a person who is raising or helping to raise a child.
- Children may be referred to either as *he* or *she*.
- *Your child* can also mean *your children*.
- Parts 1, 2, and 4 talk about children at all ages. Part 3 is about children at specific ages.

# Raising a Child

An easy formula for raising a child would be wonderful. But there is no simple guide to parenting. Kids are all different, and their needs keep changing as they grow and develop.

Parents are different, too. They have different values and different ideas of what is important.

Parents always have to be very careful with babies and toddlers. This stage of a child's life can be tiring for a parent. The parent must prevent danger and injury all the time. But at least the parent has some control over the child's world.

What happens when children get a little older? They go to school. They play on their own, with friends they choose. They make many of their own choices. And they are exposed to new kinds of danger.

Parents can't always be with their children. But you can teach your child to take care of himself. You can teach him to be self-confident.

Self-confident children tend to
- think for themselves and use common sense
- solve problems
- keep themselves safe when you're not there
- have values that stay with them as they grow

It doesn't matter that parents and families are different. There are still some things that all children need to make them self-confident. These include love and limits.

Your child needs you to understand him and be patient. He needs you to protect him and give firm guidance. He needs a good role model. That role model is you.

> Raising a self-confident, self-reliant child takes time. Your attitude as a parent is the key part.

This book can give you ideas and tips. The guidelines in it can help you keep your child safe. They can help you both be self-confident.

But remember, you know your kids best. Enjoy them. And trust yourself. If you are a self-confident parent, you'll probably raise a self-confident child.

# The Safe Child

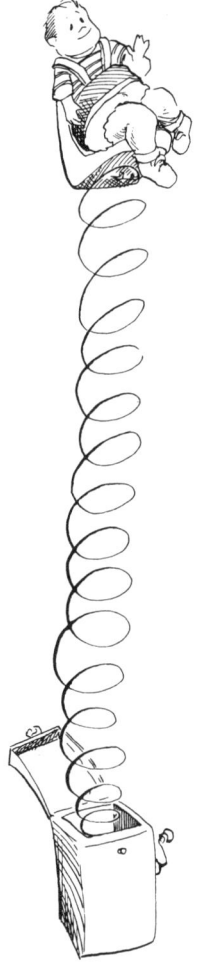

## Chapter 1
# Preventing Accidents

In the early years, your child's safety is in your hands. As they grow, kids learn what will hurt them and what will not. But in the beginning they depend on you to keep them safe. You need to protect them.

More children over one year of age die from injuries than from all illnesses combined. The three top causes of death are

- cars
- fires and burns
- drowning

*Preventing Accidents*

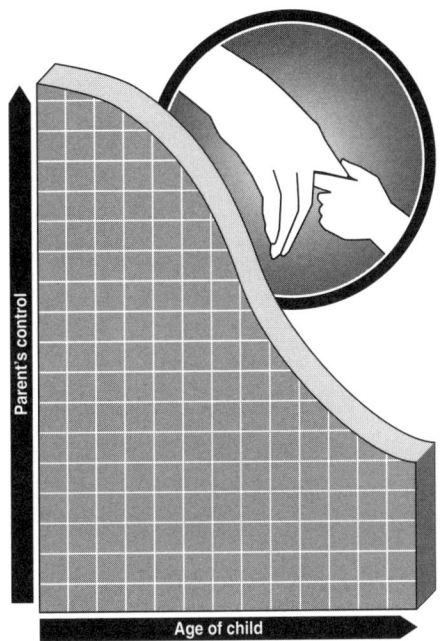

You can prevent injuries and deaths in two important ways. First, be aware of hazards and remove them. Second, watch your young child carefully. Never leave him alone.

There are times when accidents are more likely to happen. These may be

- early in the day, before parents get up
- late at night, when parents are tired or busy
- when children are hungry or tired
- when children are in new places
- when children have new routines

These are times when you need to be even more careful.

## Vehicles

Vehicles (mostly cars) cause the largest number of child deaths. Have strict rules around cars:

- Always strap your baby or small child into a car seat.
- Make older children wear seat belts—and wear one yourself.
- Never allow your child to play in a driveway or in the street. Try to find a safe place, such as a park.
- Teach your child traffic rules.
- Always make your child wears a helmet when riding a bike.
- Be sure your child's bike has reflectors if she rides at night.

## Fires and Burns

Burns are the second-largest cause of death in children. Here are some safety tips to prevent fires and burns:

- Install smoke detectors in your home. If you rent, ask your landlord to do it. Test the detectors every six months.

*Preventing Accidents* 13

- Keep a fire extinguisher in your kitchen and learn how to use it.
- Teach children to leave the building if they smell smoke.
- Keep matches away from children.
- Never leave a child alone in a room with a fire in a woodstove or a fireplace.
- Turn your hot water heater down to 120–125 degrees.
- Test the temperature of bathwater before your child gets in it.
- Use the back burners of the stove. Turn all pot handles to the back of the stove.

- Don't store cookies, candy, or other things a child might want near the stove.
- Put electrical outlet covers (from hardware stores) on all unused outlets.
- Don't leave electrical items plugged in near a bathtub, sink, or shower. They can be dangerous even if they are not turned on.
- Don't hold a child when you drink something hot.
- Iron clothes when your child is asleep or with another adult.
- Be sure curtains and bedding are not against a heater.
- Use a night-light that has a cover to protect the bulb.
- Don't use tablecloths that a child can pull off the table.

## Sunburn

The sun can burn. Even on cloudy days, about 80 percent of the sun's rays get through. Protect your child with a hat and long sleeves. For children older than 6 months, use waterproof sunblock lotion or sunscreen with a sun protection factor (SPF) of 15 or higher.

*Preventing Accidents*

## Drowning

Drowning is the third most common cause of death in young children. More small children drown in the bathtub than anywhere else. A child can drown in the time it takes to answer the door or the telephone. Here are some safety tips to prevent drowning:

- Never leave a child of 5 or younger alone in the bathtub.
- Don't leave bathwater standing in your tub.
- Keep toilet seat covers down and diaper pails closed.
- Keep an eye on a child who is swimming. Try to have an adult in the water, too.
- Put life jackets on babies and small children who can't swim.

- Never use floating toys instead of life jackets.
- Insist your child stay near someone else in the water.

## Poisoning

Many children are harmed or killed by poisons. Twenty percent of the poison accidents in the U.S. happen to 2-year-olds.

Keep all harmful chemicals out of your child's reach. These include common items like medicines, insect sprays, and cleaning supplies. Here are some safety tips to prevent poisoning:

- Have your water and paint tested to be sure they are free of lead. Call your county health department for advice about testing for lead.

  If your water pipes have lead in them, run the water for a full minute before you use it. If the paint has lead in it, ask your county health department what to do.
- Don't let your child play with plants. Over 700 plants can cause illness or death. They include many common household plants.
- Keep the phone number of the poison control center by your phone.

*Preventing Accidents* 17

- Don't take anything harmful out of the bottle it came in. If you put it in a smaller jar or cup, your child is more likely to eat or drink it.
- Keep the labels on medicines. Always follow directions for use.
- Never tell your child that medicine or vitamins are candy.
- Don't buy cleaning products that have spicy or fruity scents.
- Store all laundry and cleaning products on a high shelf or in a locked cabinet.

## Falls

Falls cause many injuries. The most common falls are from walkers and high chairs. Here are some safety tips to prevent falls:

- Make sure your child is strapped into his feeding table or high chair.

- Watch your child if he is in a walker.
- Be sure that strollers have safety straps and that you use them.
- Put up safety gates at stairs. Keep all stairways clear of toys, clothes, and other items.
- Don't put electric cords where your child could trip over them.
- Don't allow your toddler to run while eating or while carrying objects that could hurt her if she fell.
- Use a rubber bath mat in the tub.
- Babies are slippery when wet. Be careful when you lift your child out of the tub.

## Choking

Small children who are learning to eat sometimes choke. Learn how to prevent choking and what to do if choking happens:

- Don't give your child hard, round foods like nuts, candies, or raw carrot. Cut grapes and hot dogs into small pieces.
- Never leave a small child alone with objects that have small pieces.
- Only give your child toys with pieces that are too big to swallow.
- Don't let your baby drink a bottle while lying down.

*Preventing Accidents* 19

- Don't tie anything around your baby's neck except a bib. Only use a bib when the baby is strapped into a chair.
- If your child is choking, do the Heimlich maneuver.

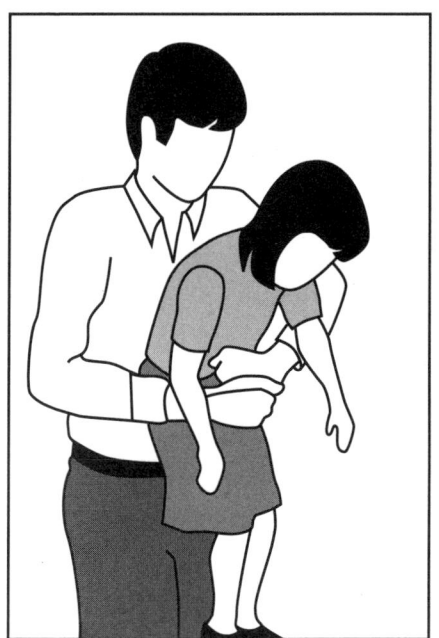

## Heimlich maneuver

1. Stand behind the child. Put your arms around her waist.
2. Place one fist between the child's ribs and belly button. Cover your fist with the other hand.
3. Give four strong upward thrusts.

## Chapter 2
# Making Your Home Safe

Many accidents happen in the home. Many of them are easy to prevent. Take a good look around your home.

There are many things you can do to make your home a safer place for a baby or small child.

Here are some tips:
- Make sure your child cannot lock herself in the bathroom.
- Don't use glass objects in the bathroom.

## Making Your Home Safe

- Put safety locks on doors and drawers that your child should not open. You can buy these locks at hardware stores.
- Cover electrical outlets. Keep all cords out of reach.
- Clear all low shelves of objects like matches, lighters, and items made of glass.
- Place freestanding shelves away from where kids play. Kids can pull these over onto themselves.
- Use fabric or tape to cover sharp edges on furniture. Remove loose tacks, staples, or buttons from stuffed furniture.
- Push chairs under tables or desks to stop children from climbing up on them.
- Keep sharp or small items like scissors, needles, pins, and buttons out of reach.

- Make sure your child's toys have no sharp edges, small pieces, cords, or strings. Make sure they are well made, won't break, and have no lead paint or toxic materials.
- Keep plastic bags and plastic wrap out of your child's reach. Tie knots in plastic bags before you throw them away. Keep balloons out of your house.
- A slippery floor is dangerous. Clean up spills right away, and remove slippery rugs.
- Don't keep guns or weapons in the house. If you must have a gun, keep it unloaded and in pieces. Store bullets separately.
- Keep a list of emergency numbers by the phone. Include your doctor, the fire department, police, poison control center, and nearest emergency room or hospital.

## Baby-Sitters

Sometimes you will leave your child in someone else's care. Always choose a trusted adult or mature teen. The person needs to be able to keep your child safe. Here are some tips to help the sitter do a good job:

- Have a new sitter meet your child or children ahead of time.
- Give a new sitter a tour of your home.

*Making Your Home Safe*

- Tell a sitter what feeding, bathing, and sleeping routines your children follow.
- Show the sitter where you keep a flashlight and first-aid supplies.
- Be sure the sitter knows that her job is to watch the children. Phone calls and TV should wait until the children are in bed.
- Show the sitter your emergency phone list. A sample is shown below. Also give him a number where he can reach you.

| Emergency Phone Numbers | |
|---|---|
| fire department | 911 |
| police | 911 |
| ambulance | 911 |
| family doctor | 000-0000 |
| poison control center | 000-0000 |
| neighbors and relatives | 000-0000 |
| | 000-0000 |
| | 000-0000 |
| local crisis hotline | 000-0000 |

## Chapter 3
# Preventing Illness

## Vaccines

Your child needs to be protected from some serious illnesses. Every child needs to be given a series of vaccines. These begin during the first six months of life. This is called vaccination or immunization. The chart on page 25 shows the shots your child needs.

Vaccinations are often given free or at a low cost at health clinics. If you don't have a family doctor or pediatrician, call your local social services agency or county health department.

(Look in the yellow pages under Social and Human Services or Health Services.) Ask about shot clinics for children.

| Vaccine | Prevents |
| --- | --- |
| DPT | diphtheria, pertussis (whooping cough), and tetanus |
| OPV | polio |
| HIB | a disease that can lead to meningitis |
| MMR | measles, mumps, and rubella (German measles) |
| HB | hepatitis B |

## Usual vaccination schedule

The chart on page 26 is a guideline for when your child needs each shot. You can get more information from a doctor or at a shot clinic.

Keep a written record of all your child's shots. You need the record:
- if your child is injured
- if your child goes to day care
- when your child starts school
- if you move
- if you change doctors

## Vaccination Schedule

Note: These guidelines sometimes change. If your child did not get all these shots, check with your doctor or pediatrician. She can give you current information and help you decide what to do.

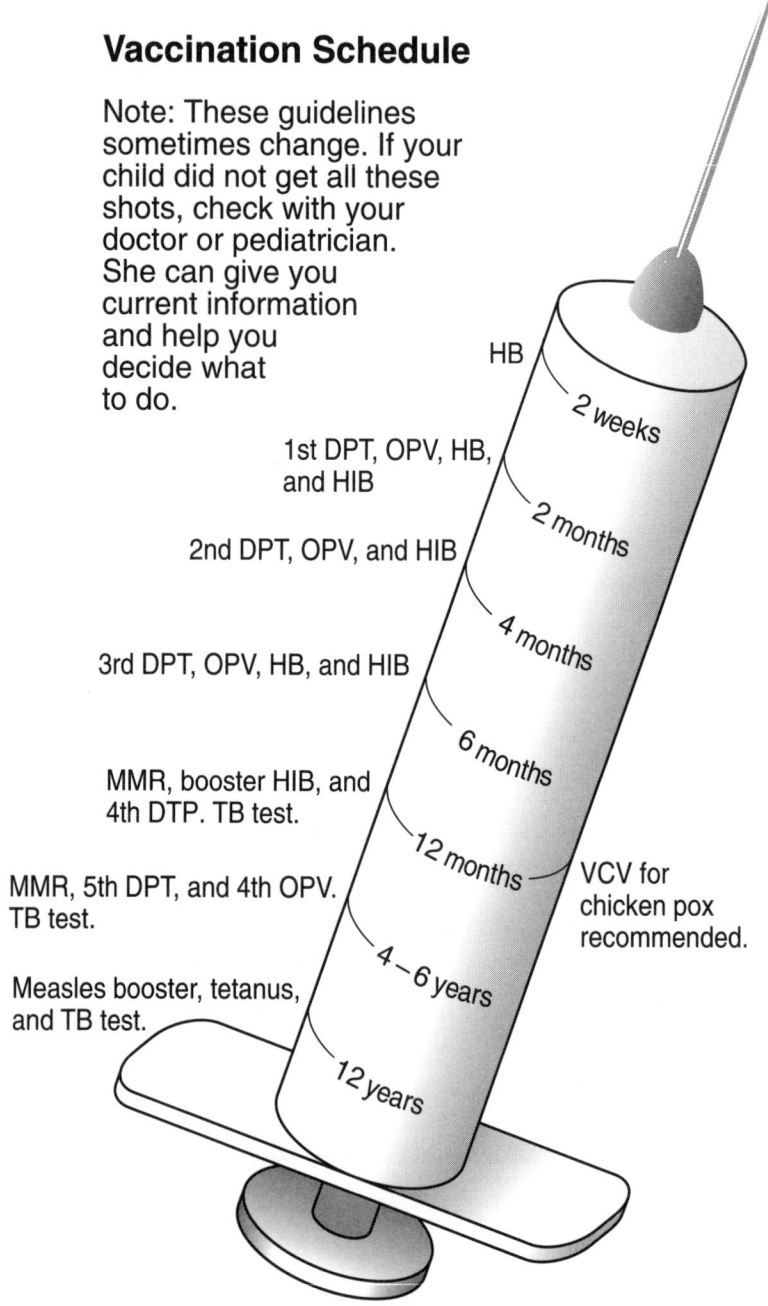

- HB — 2 weeks
- 1st DPT, OPV, HB, and HIB — 2 months
- 2nd DPT, OPV, and HIB — 4 months
- 3rd DPT, OPV, HB, and HIB — 6 months
- MMR, booster HIB, and 4th DTP. TB test. — 12 months
- MMR, 5th DPT, and 4th OPV. TB test. — 4–6 years
- Measles booster, tetanus, and TB test. — 12 years

VCV for chicken pox recommended.

*Preventing Illness* 27

Be honest about shots with an older child. Admit that the shot might hurt. Tell her that it will hurt a lot less than the disease it is preventing. If your child cries, comfort her.

Your doctor will tell you about any side effects of a shot. Sometimes there is a fever or soreness. A small lump may form where the shot was given. This is nothing to worry about.

## Checkups

Besides shots, kids need regular checkups. These are sometimes called well-baby visits or well-child visits. The doctor checks the child's health. She also checks to make sure the child is growing properly.

Ask your doctor when your baby or child should be seen. The chart on page 28 gives the ages when most babies and children should visit the doctor.

If you don't have a doctor, call your local health department. Ask about well-child clinics.

You can take these steps to keep your kids healthy. Keeping kids healthy is part of keeping them safe.

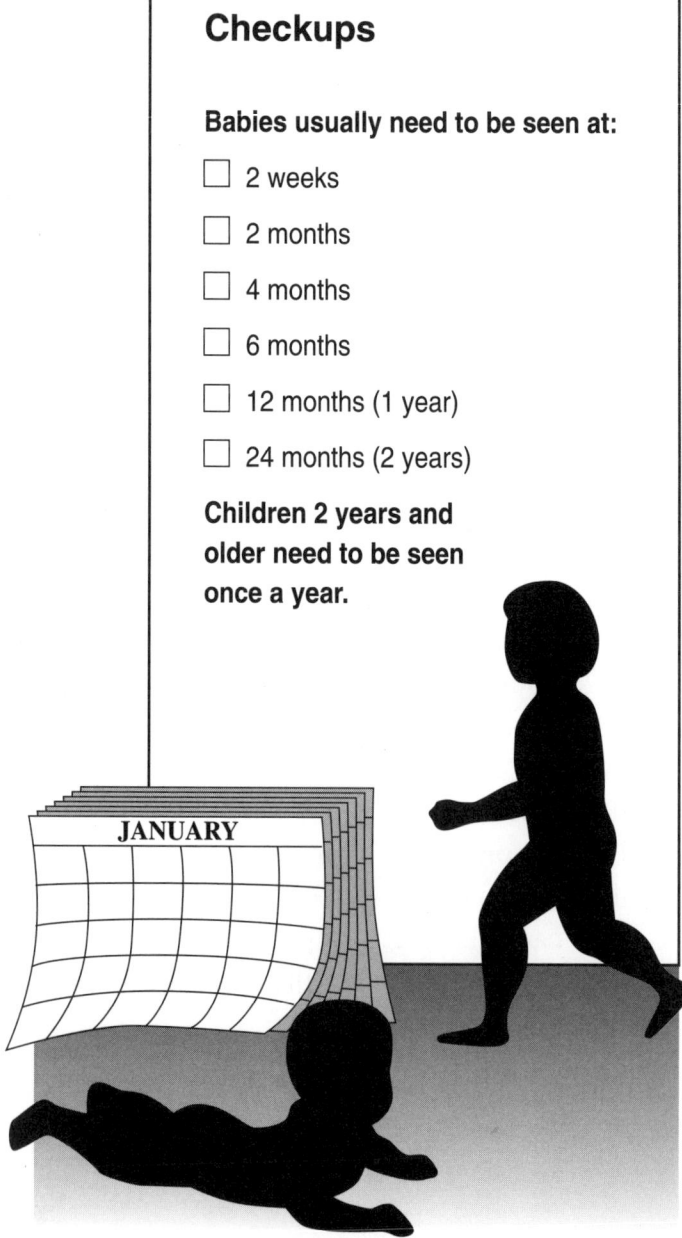

## Checkups

**Babies usually need to be seen at:**

☐ 2 weeks

☐ 2 months

☐ 4 months

☐ 6 months

☐ 12 months (1 year)

☐ 24 months (2 years)

**Children 2 years and older need to be seen once a year.**

# The Self-Confident Child

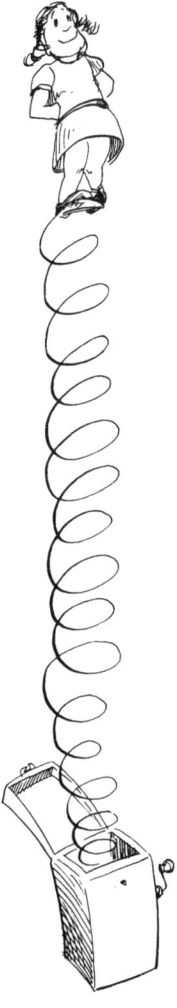

## Chapter 4
# The Right Attitude

Children have different needs at different ages. What works one day may change the next. But you and your child can keep a healthy relationship. You need to be positive and supportive.

All children need love. Remind your child often that you love him. Show him with hugs. Tell him you're proud of him.

But love is not all that children need. They also need firm limits. They should not be allowed to hurt others or make constant demands.

## The Right Attitude

Spoiled children are not happy children. They will have a hard time getting along in the world. And if you let your child be too demanding, you will get worn out and angry. That will make the problem worse.

---
You need to keep control over the important things. Let your child make choices on other things.

---

Children need to know what their limits are. Limits are the rules you set for your child. Limits are not about control. They are ways of teaching your child about himself. They are rules that teach.

Think of the word **LIMIT** like this:

## Love

Above all, no matter what. At any age, at any difficult stage. Show your child you love her. Make sure you tell her, too. Comfort her when she needs it. Hug her a lot.

## Involve

Make your child a part of your day and your life. Tell him about things you do. Don't be afraid to talk about minor problems you have. Be involved in your child's life, too. Listen carefully to what he says. Treat him like a person.

## Model

Set a good example. Don't expect your child to behave in ways you don't. Your actions have the biggest impact on how she will act. Your child will notice what you do and copy you.

## Inform

Inform yourself and your child as much as you can. Pay attention to the world around you both. Give your child the information he needs to do well in the world.

## Talk

Talk to your child as much as you possibly can. Listen carefully to what she says. Start good communication early. It's the key to preventing problems later on.

If you stick to these LIMITs, you are treating your child with love and respect.

> When you treat your child with respect, you are teaching her to respect herself. You are also teaching her to respect you.

It is never too early to adopt an attitude of respect. It does not mean letting your child control your household. It means letting your child know she is valuable. If your child feels valued, she has taken the first step to self-confidence.

## Chapter 5
# Guidance

Communication means both listening and talking. Talking and listening are *always* important. For a healthy relationship, parents and children need to talk and listen to each other. It helps children develop self-confidence. And it lets parents learn about safety problems right away.

## Guiding Your Child

Start by being clear about the things you expect. You want to guide, not punish your child. What is the difference? The chart on page 35 contrasts guidance and punishment.

| Guidance | Punishment |
|---|---|
| Says, "Stop. Do something else instead." | Threatens and demands that your child obey. |
| Focuses on the act, not the child. | Tells a child, "You are bad." |
| Sets up ways to have success next time. | Focuses on failure. |
| Comes from thought, love, and a wish for your child to be a good person. | Comes from anger. |
| Has a better chance of working because it is based on respect. | Is based on power—you are bigger and stronger than your child. |
| Lets the child learn from the logical results of behavior. | Makes the child pay for wrong behavior. |
| Allows your child to learn from his actions. | May work for a while, but makes your child angry and resentful. |
| Lets your child know that he can make good decisions. | Makes your child feel powerless. As he grows, he will obey less and less. |

## How to handle anger

If you are angry with your child, take time to cool off. Wait until your anger is under control before dealing with your child.

Your anger does not make you a bad parent. But you must find ways to release your anger without hurting your child.

Leave the room. Stomp on the floor. Pound a pillow. Cry. Yell. Clean the house.

After you let off steam safely, do something quiet to calm yourself. Breathe deeply. Count to 20. Sip a hot drink. Call a friend.

Go back to your child only when you are truly calm.

This kind of anger happens to all parents sometimes. If you find yourself being angry most of the time, however, you are suffering from too much strain.

You deserve expert help. Call a local crisis hot line if there is one. Check the front of your phone book, or call Directory Assistance. Or ask someone—a doctor, social worker, clergy, relative, or friend—where you can get help.

## Listening to your upset child

Children feel valued and loved when you listen to them. By listening you give them a chance to solve their own problems.

Guidance

Listening is a skill that can be improved. When you listen well, you hear what your child says. You also see how she feels. And you don't give quick advice.

Listening to an upset child can be hard for parents. Look at what the parent in this picture is saying to her upset child.

Such responses don't often help. Your child needs you to listen, not scold or comfort.

> Don't you dare talk to me like that!
> You shouldn't feel that way.
> It can't be that bad.
> I told you that would happen.
> What did you expect?
> You'll feel better soon.

To listen well, stop what you are doing. Look your child in the eye. Tune into what you see and hear.

Say things that show you are listening. Ask questions about what you hear. Nod your head. This shows you want her to keep talking. Look at the parent's responses below.

Responses like these are called "open responses." They show you care. They do not take over the problem or give advice.

> It seems like you had a tough day.
> Uh-huh.
> Why don't you tell me about it?
> What can I do to help?
> I see.

Open responses allow your child to get her feelings out. Then she can be calm and ready to think about solving her own problem.

## Asking your child questions

Guiding your child takes more than listening. It also means asking questions.

> Asking questions can show you are interested in your child. It is also a way to get information that the child doesn't bring up on his own.

It takes practice to ask good questions. Questions can be closed or open, like responses. Open questions help the flow of communication. Closed questions can limit the flow.

One kind of closed question asks for a simple yes or no answer. "Are you still having trouble with your homework?"

Questions that start with "Why?" are usually closed. "Why didn't you start your homework sooner?" Your child may feel that you are accusing him of something.

Open questions work better. They ask in a way that lets your child share his concerns or ideas. "How is the homework going?"

Your tone of voice must also show you are interested in your child's point of view.

Even open questions won't work unless you listen to your child's answers without judging. Give advice only when your child asks for it. Questioning and listening go hand in hand. And both take practice.

## Talking to your child

Guiding your child takes listening well and asking good questions. Sharing your feelings and needs is also important.

Talk about good things your child has done. Praise her successes. Praise her efforts, too.

Sometimes your child's behavior may cause a problem for you. You and your child need to talk about the problem. Choose a calm time.

Avoid "you-messages." These are statements that focus on the child and accuse her. *"You never come to meals on time."*

Use "I-messages" to talk about the problem. I-messages focus on how *you* feel and why you feel that way. *"I get upset when I cook dinner and you are not here to share it."*

There are no orders in I-messages. They show respect for your child. I-messages appeal to your child's good nature. In most cases, she knows what needs to be done.

What if you listen well, ask open questions, and send I-messages, but the problem still remains? What can you do?

First, deal with the problem when you are feeling calm. If you are angry, you may

- accuse and blame the child
  *"How can you be so difficult?"*
- overgeneralize
  *"I can never count on you."*
- lecture or preach
  *"I'm only looking out for your own good."*
- command or threaten
  *"If you don't stop that this minute, you'll be in big trouble."*

Those angry responses will not help you and your child solve a problem.

When you are calm, check to see if you and your child understand the problem.

**State problem**

*She comes home late. You have told her that you worry that she may be hurt or in trouble. She is annoyed because she thinks you are too protective.*

Explore some ways to solve the problem. Ask your child to think of solutions. Accept all the ideas that she comes up with. Don't comment or judge. If you have more ideas, add them.

Gather all the ideas you can. Then ask your child to choose a plan of action that you can agree with.

**Agreed-upon solution**

*Perhaps you will allow her to stay out a half hour later. She agrees not to be more than 15 minutes late. If something unusual happens to delay her, she will call.*

Together, agree on what will happen if she fails to follow the plan of action.

**Result if not followed**

*She will not be allowed to go out in the evening for a week.*

It is important to agree on the result if she doesn't follow the plan. And it is important to enforce the result if you need to.

Ask her to follow the plan of action for a set period (perhaps two weeks). Agree to check at the end of that time to see if it is working. Agree to try another solution if it is not.

Children often accept solutions when they share in creating them.

### Let them solve it

Parenting is a long process of letting go. You want your child to learn to function on his own. Your job is to love him and let him go. You can't succeed with punishment and threats.

Many parents complain that they have to nag or punish. Otherwise, the child doesn't do homework, pick up toys, or get up in time.

Let your child learn to handle his own problems. Ask yourself, "Does this problem interfere with me? Does it affect my child's safety?" If the answers are no, don't make the problem yours.

### Comparing

Let your child develop at her own pace. Don't compare her—at any age—to other children or babies.

If you are worried that she is not developing, check with a doctor. Otherwise, let her be herself. Celebrate each new thing she learns to do. Let her know you're proud of her successes.

## Misbehavior

Some children misbehave a lot. If your child does, try to find out why.

Kids misbehave for many reasons:

- looking for attention

    Do you feel annoyed? Your child may be seeking attention. When you are annoyed, he gets attention for the wrong thing. Try to ignore the action. And give him more attention at other times.

- struggling for power
  Do you feel angry? You may be in a power struggle with your child. Your anger adds to the struggle. Don't stay and fight. Walk away.
- seeking revenge
  Do you feel hurt? Your child may be trying to get back at you for some reason. Don't pressure him, even if you feel hurt.
- proving "I'm no good."
  Do you feel hopeless? Children who have been blamed and criticized a lot may feel that they can't do anything. They act in ways that "prove" they can't do anything right.

Do not call your child "bad" when you stop his misbehavior. Praise him for his effort and improvement whenever you can. Talk about his good points to him and in front of him to others.

The above examples all suggest what may be causing your child's misbehavior. And they all suggest that you, the parent, must change. Most parents are surprised to learn that to stop their child's misbehavior, *they* must change.

If your child misbehaves a lot, you may want some help. Parenting classes can give you a chance to practice new skills. They can also help you know that you are not alone in dealing with problems. To find out about parenting classes, ask at your public library, doctor's office, county health department, social services department, or place of worship.

## Chores

Children need to develop skills in taking care of themselves and their living space. From an early age, they can have regular chores to do. They can wash dishes, sort laundry, set the table, or tidy their own areas. Teach them how to do this.

Taking part in running the home can help kids feel valuable. Learning skills gives them confidence. It teaches them to be responsible.

## Chapter 6

# How Are You Doing?

Are you helping your child to become self-confident? Do you need to change anything? You can take the self-tests on pages 48–50 to see how you are doing.

The two self-tests will help you find out

- if you're spending enough time with your child
- if you're paying enough attention to her

## Self-Test

**How are you guiding your child?**

Check "Yes," "No," or "Sometimes" for each of the following questions.

|  | Yes | No | Sometimes |
|---|---|---|---|
| Do you change the rules often? | ___ | ___ | ___ |
| Do you change rules without talking about the change first? | ___ | ___ | ___ |
| Do you ever make promises you can't keep? | ___ | ___ | ___ |
| Do you ever threaten to do something and then not do it? | ___ | ___ | ___ |
| Do you do things for your child that she could do for herself? | ___ | ___ | ___ |
| Do you correct your child in front of other people? | ___ | ___ | ___ |

Did you answer "Yes" or "Sometimes" to any of these questions? You may want to think about changing how you do those things.

# ✓ Self-Test

## How well do you know your child?

See if you can answer all these questions. Then go over them with your child to see if you were right.

**What is your child's favorite**

food _____

color _____

song _____

animal _____

TV show _____

toy or game _____

book _____

person _____

time to be alone _____

holiday _____

**What makes your child**

happy _____

sad _____

mad _____

## Self-Test, continued

excited _____

scared _____

proud _____

**Where does your child**

play indoors _____

play outdoors _____

like to go _____

like to eat out _____

If you got most of the questions right, you've been paying attention to your child. Your child probably has self-confidence.

If you got many of them wrong, you may need to pay more attention to your child. Spend more time together. Listen more to her. Find activities you like to do together.

Celebrate special days like birthdays. Celebrate special moments such as when she gets a good grade. Let her know you're proud of her successes.

# 3

# Special Ages, Special Needs

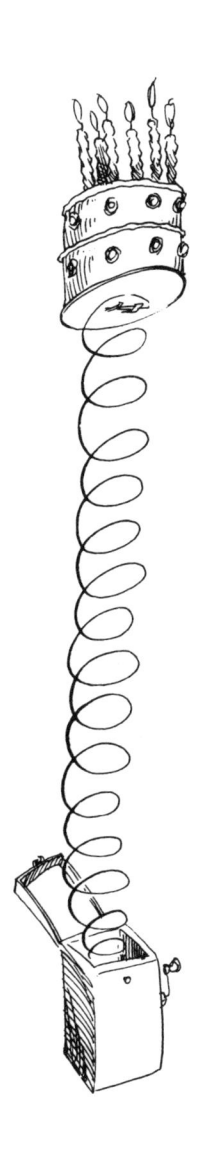

## Chapter 7
# Babies

Babies are learning a lot during their first six months. They pay attention to human sounds. They like to look at faces and eyes.

As soon as they are born, babies begin to trust and form a sense of self. Parents who care for a baby with love will bond with him. The baby will feel the love, and will bond too.

Bonding is the start of a lifelong link between parent and child. To bond, babies need to be hugged, held, touched, and cuddled. Talk to your baby as often as you can. Sing to him.

Play with him. Read to him. Give your baby things to look at, listen to, touch, smell, and taste. Handle him gently.

Babies cry for many reasons. They may be wet, thirsty, cold, or hot. They may need to burp or suck. They could be tired or sick. Or they may be bored or overexcited.

Don't be alarmed if your baby cries. Some babies have long crying spells even though you try to make them feel better. Many babies fuss most during the evening.

Perhaps the baby does not behave as you expected. Maybe the baby has colic and cries for hours at a time. Some babies do not sleep much at night. They keep their parents up a lot.

New parents don't expect to get cross with their newborn. But when they are tired and stressed, they may not be able to stop themselves.

If your baby is fussy, try to make him comfortable. Here are some ideas: rock him, take him for a walk or ride, listen to music, turn off the lights, or give him a bath.

If your baby won't be comforted and you become angry, put him down in a safe place. Leave the room for a minute or two. Read the tips for handling anger on page 36.

When you are taking care of a newborn full-time, it is important to take care of yourself. Another adult may be able to give you a break from time to time. Or when your baby is napping, give yourself a break. Do something you like to do.

## From 6 Months to 1 Year

Separation begins when a baby is between 6 months and 1 year old. When your baby is born, she depends on you for everything. But she starts to separate at a young age. At about 6 months she wants less cuddling. She struggles to sit up. She tries to hold things for herself.

Encourage your baby. If she shows independence, be proud of her. If she needs extra cuddling, enjoy it. Respond to her needs.

### Checklist for a safe baby

- Use a safe crib. Be sure your baby's head cannot fit between the slats. Crib bars should be no more than 3 fingers apart.

- Keep the sides of your baby's crib locked and in the highest position.
- Do not leave plastic bags or plastic wrap near the baby.
- Lay your baby down in safe places where she can't fall.
- Keep a hand on your baby when changing diapers. Never leave your baby alone when you are changing or bathing her.
- Give your baby safe toys. There should be no sharp edges or small parts.
- Keep small and sharp objects out of reach.
- Don't play rough with your baby.
- Don't hold your baby while eating or drinking hot things or smoking.

## Checklist for a self-confident baby

- Remember the LIMITs on page 32.
- Breast-feed your baby if you can. If you bottle-feed, cuddle him when he is eating.
- Keep your baby fed, warm, and dry.
- Go to your baby quickly when he cries.
- Smile often at your baby, and look him in the eye.
- Touch and caress your baby gently.
- Talk or sing to your baby.

- Give your baby lots of chances to see objects of different colors and shapes.
- Let your baby touch things. He needs to learn how things feel: wet and dry, soft and hard, smooth and rough, light and heavy, cool and warm.

## Chapter 8
# Toddlers (Ages 1-3)

## From 1 to 2 Years Old

One-year-olds are explorers. They no longer stay in one place. They crawl. They like to climb onto things and fit into things.

They poke, shake, lift, and taste everything they can get to. This is how they learn about the world. By getting into everything, babies find out about the size, shape, taste, and weight of things. This is important for their development.

At home, remove most things your baby should not play with. Leave plenty of things it is OK for her to touch. Let her touch and get to know objects that are not harmful.

Babies this age will get some cuts and bruises as part of their active play. You cannot prevent all injuries. But you must protect your child from serious harm. Chapters 1 and 2 of this book give you tips on how to do that.

Some 1-year-olds become afraid of sudden noises or motions, such as those of vacuum cleaners. Try to let your baby get used to things a little at a time, and from a distance.

Babies this age will crawl away from their parent to explore. But they also return often to feel secure. As time goes by, babies go farther and stay away longer. They become more outgoing with people besides their parents.

Let your baby learn all she can at this age. Give her freedom to explore, even if she gets dirty. But stop her from eating dirt and trash.

## Eating

As babies grow older they change their eating habits. Some babies become more picky and less hungry. Don't worry if this happens. If you offer only good foods, your child will still be getting a healthy diet.

Toddlers need the same kinds of good foods as adults—fruits, vegetables, breads, cereals, and proteins, such as milk, meat, fish, eggs, and cheese.

Children this age want to feed themselves. Be prepared to handle the mess. Feed your child in his own chair. Use bowls, plates, and cups that will not break. Use a bib.

The mess is sometimes annoying. But what the child learns helps him develop confidence. It helps him become independent.

Try to keep mealtime happy. Feed your baby before he is too hungry. That way, he'll be more relaxed. Take your time, if you can. Smile and talk to your baby at mealtime.

## Learning language

Babies try to make the sounds they hear. At about 12 months, they may say their first word.

You don't need to teach language. Just talk to your baby or toddler a lot as you care for her. Read to her as part of your playtime. Say words correctly and clearly, not in "baby talk."

Your child will pronounce some words wrong. Some sounds will be hard for her to say. Don't scold or try to teach the word. Your child wants to copy. She will learn faster if you don't make a fuss.

## Teaching *no*

There are always some things babies and toddlers must leave alone, like electrical outlets. At first, you can't stop your child by just saying *no*. You must teach him that *no* means something.

Try to be patient with your child. Defying you helps him discover who he is. Be firm, however. You want your child to know what is an important *no:* "No, don't touch the stove." He needs to know the difference between this and a *no* that does not matter as much: "No, don't touch Mommy's magazine."

## Bedtime

Keep bedtime happy if you can. Try not to rush it. Try to keep to a regular routine your child knows—like bath, diaper change, song, and good-night kiss. Then leave.

If your child is afraid, don't leave him alone in the dark. A night-light or other light left on may help. Try to help him feel comfortable at bedtime.

## From 2 to 3 Years Old

Perhaps you've heard the saying "the terrible twos." Between 2 and 3 years old, children don't care much about pleasing others. They are too busy becoming themselves. They often cannot even please themselves. They have a hard time making up their minds. Then, when they do, they change them again.

Kids this age are bossy. They say no a lot. They insist on doing things their own way. They become angry when someone moves their things around.

Your 2-year-old is not being bad. She is becoming independent in the only way she knows how. Keep telling yourself things will be better soon.

Toddlers learn by copying others. They become angry when they can't do what older kids are doing. But they don't want help. Try not to interfere. And try not to hurry your child.

Dressing is one example. Toddlers often want to dress themselves. You need to be very patient. If you don't help at all, your child may never get dressed. And if you help too much or hurry her, she gets angry.

Give only as much help as your toddler needs. Some tasks will be too hard for her. Get her interested in a toy or an easy job while you do the harder ones.

## Play

Children love to play. When they play, they also learn. They find out how the world works. They learn to use their bodies with skill. They practice solving problems. They develop confidence.

At first children don't play much with each other. But they like to watch what other children are doing.

Let children play at their own level. For young children, simple toys are best. They allow kids to develop imagination.

Let your child pretend. He may dress up in your old clothes or have a pretend friend. He may pretend to be an animal.

Most children enjoy playing with dolls. Both boys and girls should be allowed to do so. Such play can help children act out their own feelings about things. It can also help children develop caring feelings for others.

Plan some time for your child to color, paint with a brush, or fingerpaint. Give your child big pieces of paper. Let him draw or scribble whatever he likes. Be prepared for a mess. Have your child wear old clothes or give him an apron.

Toddlers usually love music. Let your child march or dance to music on the radio. Play music whenever you can. Sing together.

## Learning limits

It's OK to insist on some limits to what toddlers do. You don't want your child to hit another child on the head, for example.

You need to be both firm and friendly when you stop a toddler's bad behavior. Let your child know that it is OK to feel angry. But it is not OK to grab, bite, kick, or hit because she is angry.

Don't try to talk a small child out of bad behavior. Stop the action. Show clearly that you won't accept the behavior. Don't give too many reasons; children this age can't listen to reason. Be prepared, however, for your child to be angry when you stop her from doing something. Expect her to cry or scream.

It takes a lot of patience to handle a child this age. Parents who aren't rushed and aren't too bossy seem to do best.

Parents need to take care of themselves. Otherwise, they may threaten, scold, or punish their toddler a lot. If that happens to you, seek some help. Places to get help are included in Part 4, pages 95–96.

## Tips for handling toddlers

- Give your child only one simple direction or warning at a time.
- Distract your child if you see a problem developing. Offer an activity or toy that will get his interest.

- Don't ask your child if he wants to do something unless he really has a choice.
- Give your child lots of chances to choose between two things that you are willing to let him do. "Do you want to read a book or play with the truck?"

- Go matter-of-factly through regular routines. Don't say "*It's time for lunch—OK?*" or "*Shall we put your coat on now?*" This just gives your child a chance to say no.
- Find ways to say yes to your child. You can do this without giving him exactly what he wants. Instead of "*No, you can't have a cookie,*" say "*Yes, you can have a cookie after lunch.*"
- Sometimes your child must wait for your attention. Tell him when you will be with him in a way that he can understand. Say "*I will play with you after I finish washing the dishes*" not "*in a minute*" or "*after a while*" or "*soon.*"

## Toilet training

Be relaxed about toilet training. Try not to hurry or pressure your child. When she starts showing interest, she is ready to begin. Any time between 2 and 3 years old is normal. Here are some tips for toilet training:

- Praise your child for success.
- Treat accidents calmly.
- Show your child how much paper to use for wiping.

- Help your child wash her hands after using the toilet.
- To help a child stay dry at night, do not give her drinks in the evening. Have her use the toilet just before going to bed.
- Leave some light in the bathroom at night.

## Checklist for a safe toddler

- Never leave your child alone.
- Be sure baby-sitters watch your child closely.
- Make your home safe. Chapter 2, page 20, gives some tips for doing this.
- Physically remove your child from danger.

## Checklist for a self-confident toddler

- Remember the LIMITs on page 32.
- Allow your toddler to explore safe activities.
- Only say no when you need to. Be firm about stopping behavior you won't accept.
- Speak calmly to your toddler.
- Try to stick to a daily routine.

## Toddlers (Ages 1–3)

- Play with your toddler at her level.
- Let your toddler spend time around other children.
- Limit the amount of time your toddler watches TV. Be sure the content is not violent.

## Chapter 9
# Preschoolers (Ages 4-5)

Preschoolers continue to grow more independent. At this stage, they are more sure of themselves. They are not as negative as when they were toddlers. They accept your authority better.

Preschoolers want to please and copy you. They can learn manners and to say "please" and "thank you."

Allow your child to do things for herself. Now is a good time to give her a regular chore at home. She can pick up her own toys. She can set the table.

## Preschoolers (Ages 4–5)

Let your preschooler spend time with other children. She needs to learn to share and make friends.

Children this age want to know about everything. They like to have things explained. They ask "Why?" a lot. Try to be patient with your child's many questions. Answer them if you can.

Preschool children often make up stories. They like tall tales and pretend. They may not be sure of the difference between real and pretend.

Sometimes kids this age develop fears. They can be afraid of anything: the dark, dogs, strangers. They may imagine dangers they have never actually faced.

Don't make fun of your child. Don't try to argue her out of her fears. Let her talk about them.

Preschoolers play at what they see grown-ups do. They pretend they are going to work, driving a car, or taking care of a house. They may use the same words and gestures as their parents.

Children this age notice how you act with others. Do you treat your mate as boss, as helpless, or as a partner? That may affect how your child thinks about men and women. It is important to model actions you want your child to copy and learn.

What you do has a great impact on what your child will become. It is more important than what you say.

## Curious about bodies

Preschoolers often ask where babies come from, or why boys are made differently from girls. Answer your child's questions simply. Use correct words when you teach your child about body parts.

Learning about sex will take place all through childhood. It is not helpful to tell your child more than he can understand. But it is important for your child to feel that it's OK to ask. He will have other questions later.

## Strangers

The preschool years are a good time to tell your kids about strangers. It is important that they know who they can and cannot go places with.

Tell your child that a stranger is anyone she doesn't know. She should not take anything from a stranger. She should not go anywhere with a stranger.

## Preschoolers (Ages 4–5)

Your child may be shy around people you know if she doesn't know them. Tell her it is OK for her to talk to people when you are there. Don't push her. She will learn the difference as she gets older.

### Checklist for a safe preschooler

- Keep an eye on your child wherever she is—indoors or out. Have baby-sitters do this, too.

- Make your home safe. Check other places where your child spends time, too.
- Limit TV. Make sure your child isn't watching violent programs.
- Teach your child not to go anywhere with strangers, and to say no to anything that feels bad.
- Do not let your child play in the street or near traffic.
- Show your child how to be safe on a playground.
- Teach your child whom to call in an emergency (911).

## Checklist for a self-confident preschooler

- Remember the LIMITs on page 32.
- Answer your child's questions honestly and as simply as you can.
- Speak to your child the way you want him to speak.
- Make clear rules and stick to them.
- Supervise your child's play with other children.
- Correct your child's behavior without telling him he's bad.
- Try to stick to a daily routine.
- Spend time enjoying your child.

## Chapter 10
# Older Kids (Ages 6-9)

The early school years are a time of change. Children spend many hours in a new place. They learn how to get along on their own. They form new friendships.

Your 6- to 9-year-old child's world is getting bigger. You no longer have as much control over what he sees, hears, and does. He begins to see things from others' points of view. He is also developing a sense of dignity. He no longer wants you to show him off as a cute child.

Children this age go on loving their parents deeply. But they often don't show it.

At this age, children begin to wonder about big questions like life, love, the future, and death. They believe they can do or be anything. If a child likes to skate, he may think he will become a famous skater.

Listen to your child's dreams. Don't tell him how unlikely they are to come true. He will discover his limits soon enough.

It is still good for children this age to follow a routine and have a regular bedtime. Include some quiet time to talk, read, or just be with your child at bedtime, if you can.

## "Baby" habits

Some 6-year-olds find the larger world strange and scary. They return to "baby" habits like sucking their thumb for comfort. Parents often think it is time to break baby habits. They may scold or tease their child. This only makes the problem worse.

Most children will begin to drop such habits on their own. They have other things to do. They don't want to be teased by classmates. They want to be more grownup. But when the child is home and tired, she returns to her habit for comfort.

Show respect and love for your child. The less you pressure her, the less likely she is to cling to earlier habits.

## Right and wrong

By this age, you have taught your child ideas of right and wrong. These ideas have become a part of his view of the world. He may get annoyed when you keep reminding him of what he should do. He may defy you or fight with brothers and sisters. He may be very messy.

Your child had learned better behavior. Now he seems to forget it. That's partly because he is copying the actions of kids his own age.

Try to overlook some of the small irritating things your child does. He needs all the freedom and choice he can handle. You still need to let him know what you expect of him, however.

## Setting limits

Set firm limits in matters that are important to you. Make rules that are needed to keep your child safe. And make rules about behavior that you will not accept. (For example: Do not steal.)

Your child should know what will happen if she breaks a rule. Will you take away a privilege? Will you ground her for a while? Be sure to follow through with the expected result of breaking rules.

If a child begins to misbehave a lot, see if you can find a reason for it.

Look at what is going on in your child's life. Is she having a problem you don't know about? Is she finding schoolwork hard? Is there a new child in the family? Are her friends pressuring her? If you can find a reason for misbehavior, you can probably find a solution. Use the tips on pages 44 and 45.

## School

First grade is harder than preschool or kindergarten. Talk about school before your child starts. Let him ask questions. Visit the school if you can.

Make the start of school as pleasant as you can. Let your child take a small toy or special pencil to school. Give him a favorite snack.

If your child doesn't like school after a few weeks, do some checking. Sometimes the trouble comes from the school. Is the class too big? Is a teacher too harsh?

The problem may also lie with your child. There may be a physical problem. He may have poor eyesight or hearing. Maybe he has a learning problem. These things can be tested.

Maybe your child is worried about something going on at home or at school. Maybe he has a hard time paying attention.

Whatever the cause, don't punish your child if he is having trouble in school. Try to find out what the problem is. Ask for a meeting with his teacher or a school official. Share what you know and ask for their ideas. Together you can find ways to help your child.

## Homework

As children get older, they start having homework. Homework is your child's job, not yours. Don't let it become a struggle between you and your child. If she doesn't do it, she's the one who must face the teacher, not you.

You can, however, set some routines that may help your child. Let her have a snack and time for active play right after school. She needs the change of pace.

At first, stay near your child if you can while she is doing homework. Do something quiet, such as reading, sewing, or paying bills. Take a regular five-minute break with your child. Let her work in the way that seems best for her. She may need to move around, draw pictures, or read aloud while she works.

## Dangers and Safety

As your child grows, his safety may depend on his actions outside the home. You may not be around. Don't just let your child do what his friends are doing. Decide based on his skills and how dependable he is.

You can agree on some clear rules. Here is a list you can go over together:

- Always say where you are going and when you will be home.
- Walk and go places with friends.
- Use public rest rooms with a friend.
- Keep your eyes and ears open.
- Walk in the middle of the sidewalk.
- Avoid areas that are badly lit or empty.
- Stay a safe distance away if someone in a car stops to talk to you.
- Know your route. Spot safe places to go to if you need help. These may be stores, gas stations, homes of friends, or public areas.
- Never go anywhere with strangers.
- Know where there are pay phones. Always carry some change and emergency phone numbers, including your home number.
- Run from trouble or yell for help.
- If you are being followed, cross the street. Walk faster. Run if you need to. Go toward the nearest area where other people are.
- If you are being followed by someone in a car, change directions. The car will have to make a U-turn to follow you.
- If someone tries to make you try drugs, refuse.

## Sexual abuse

If someone or something makes your child feel bad, she needs to be able to say no.

Parents often fear their child will be violently attacked by a stranger. This can happen. That is why children need to be streetsmart. But more often, children are hurt by a person they know. This is often the case with sexual abuse.

Talk about touching. Tell your child what you think is OK and what is not. Ask your child what she thinks.

Abuse can start slowly. A trusted person may touch your child and say that he is only being friendly or loving. But if your child feels bad, she needs to trust her feelings.

Teach your child to say no to what makes her feel bad. And teach her to tell you about such happenings. Make it safe for your child to talk to you. Believe her.

Also look for signs of stress in your child. Is her sleep disturbed? Is there a big change in her eating? Is her behavior suddenly different? Are her grades dropping? Does she refuse to go places?

Talk with your child if you see signs of distress. Don't be afraid to get outside help if you need it.

Be aware of the dangers your child faces. Be sure you have open communication.

Don't be afraid to state your beliefs about hard subjects. Kids are in more danger if they lack information. Talk openly about drugs, AIDS, sex, and other hard topics.

Your child should get the right information from you. If she doesn't, she may get wrong information from someone else. Make sure the information *you* have is right, as well.

## Checklist for a safe child 6-9 years old

- Make sure your child is comfortable and safe by himself before you leave him alone.
- Be aware of any drug abuse around your child. Talk with him about it.
- Be sure your child knows and follows safety rules.
- Be sure your child never goes anywhere with strangers.

## Checklist for a self-confident child 6-9

- Remember the LIMITs on page 32.
- Show interest in what goes on at school.
- Help your child think about the possible results of her actions.
- When you disagree with your child, explain why.
- Invite your child's friends to your home.
- When you don't know how she feels, ask her.
- Spend time together.

## Chapter 11
# Preteens (Ages 9-12)

Preteens worry about how the world works and how they fit into it. From their successes, they learn what their skills are. From their failures, they learn what their weak areas are.

As kids gain experience in the world, they come to think their parents know nothing. They are impatient with your "old-fashioned" ideas.

They seem more concerned about what their friends think of them than what you think. They pull farther away from you.

These are signs that your child is growing normally. Give him as much freedom as he can handle. He has not forgotten the lessons you have already taught.

Young kids feel strongly about things. But their feelings change quickly. Your child's on-again, off-again emotions come partly from the rapid changes he is going through. This period is called puberty.

Growth hormones are racing through your child's body. Children may grow 12 inches and gain 20 to 30 pounds during puberty. At the same time, sexual organs are maturing.

It is normal for kids to touch or rub their sexual organs (masturbate). This is not harmful.

There is no set age at which puberty begins. Many girls begin to change as young as 10 years old, and have their first period two years later. But it is also normal for the changes to come at a younger or older age.

You need to talk with your child about body changes before they begin. Your child may be upset if he is taken by surprise. Keep on answering questions as your child asks them.

But some preteens won't say what is on their minds. They may not ask any questions. In that case, you can bring up the subject. Many magazines have articles that you can use as an opener. Some TV programs can help you bring it up. The important thing is to keep listening and talking—even about hard topics.

Boys and girls need to be told matter-of-factly about their body changes. Help them look forward to their lives as adults.

Don't limit your information to what happens to your child's own sex. Boys need to learn about girls, and girls about boys.

Don't worry if your child shows little interest or acts bored when you share this information. It is up to you to give her correct information.

*Preteens (Ages 9–12)*

Puberty is an awkward time for both boys and girls. They feel self-conscious. They worry. They are moody. They think a lot about how they look.

To make matters harder, many kids develop skin problems during puberty. Skin problems may be reduced in several ways. Your child needs to follow good health habits such as:
- getting daily exercise
- eating fruits and vegetables
- cutting down on fatty foods
- getting plenty of sleep

## Checklist for a safe child 9-12 years old

- See earlier lists in previous chapters.
- Be sure your child always tells you where she is.
- Discuss how to act with strangers.
- Discuss the dangers of drugs.

## Checklist for a self-confident child 9-12

- Remember the LIMITs on page 32.
- Tell your child about body changes in puberty.

- Tell your daughter to be proud of developing an adult body. Talk about unnatural body images of women on TV, in movies, in ads, and in magazines. Tell her that female models are paid to be thinner than is natural.
- Tell your son to be proud of developing an adult body. Tell him that male models are paid to be more muscular than is usual.
- Help your child think about the possible results of his actions.
- Talk to your child about hard topics such as drugs, sex, AIDS, abuse, and racism.
- Encourage your child's interests and activities.
- Give your child more freedom.
- Give your child harder and more interesting chores.
- Spend some time with your child doing things you both enjoy.
- Show interest in what goes on at school.
- Invite your child's friends to your home.

## Chapter 12

# Teenagers (Ages 13 and Up)

If you've gotten this far, you are almost there. The baby you once protected so carefully is now almost an adult.

Along the way, he has learned self-respect. He has also learned to think for himself. He can protect himself. And he has tools to make his way in the world and be happy.

> The close relationship you build with a safe, self-confident child can last your whole life. There is nothing more important that a parent can do.

91

## Checklist for a safe teen

- If your teen drives, have strict rules.
- Know who his friends are.
- Talk about the risks and responsibilities of sex.
- Talk about the risks of alcohol and drug use.
- Know where he is on overnight stays.
- Model responsible behavior.

## Checklist for a self-confident teen

- Remember the LIMITs on page 32.
- Show your teen respect and trust. Let her take responsibility for her actions.
- Listen to her. Solve problems together.
- Treat her like an adult. Try to get agreement on rules.
- Show your teen that she can always find love at home.
- Encourage her to bring friends home.
- Encourage your teen to question things.
- Spend some time together doing activities you both enjoy.
- Continue to show interest in what goes on at school.

# 4

# Resources

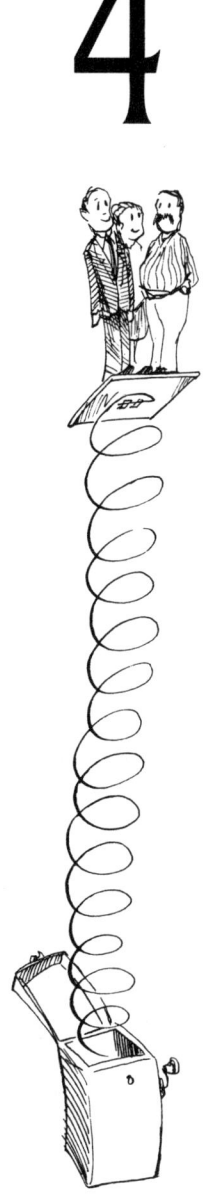

# Where to Get Help

  This book gives many tips for helping your child be safe and self-confident. But sometimes you may need outside advice.

  The chart on pages 95 and 96 gives some tips for getting this advice. The chart lists who may help. It shows what kind of support they can give. Most of the people are easy to find. You probably see them in your daily life.

  If you are in a crisis, seek help right away. A crisis might be feeling anger you can't control or feeling overwhelmed. To take good care of children, you need to take care of yourself.

|  | How they help: | Who are they? |
|---|---|---|
| **Other parents** | • tips they found that worked<br>• shared experiences<br>• support—other people have the same problems<br>• someone to talk to | • friends<br>• relatives<br>• neighbors<br>• parents of your child's friends<br>• parenting or childbirth class members |
| **Day care** | • can tell you what your child is doing while away from you<br>• give advice—they work with many kids<br>• work with you on special needs your child has (like toilet training) | • baby-sitters<br>• day care providers<br>• anyone who watches your child for you |
| **School staff** | • give advice—they are experts on kids<br>• meet with you to talk about your concerns<br>• resources available for special needs | • teachers<br>• guidance counselors<br>• administrators (like the principal)<br>• school psychologists |

|  | **How they help:** | **Who are they?** |
|---|---|---|
| **Health care providers** | • give advice—experts on kids<br>• check growth and development<br>• check for abuse if you ask | • family doctor<br>• pediatrician<br>• doctor at a health center or clinic (Call your county health department to find one.)<br>• school nurse |

|  | **How they help:** | **How to find them—Ask at your:** |
|---|---|---|
| **Parenting classes** | • training keeps you up-to-date as a parent<br>• new ideas and tips<br>• give advice—trained experts | • public library<br>• county health department<br>• social services department<br>• doctor's office<br>• place of worship |
| **Crisis help** | • listen to your concerns<br>• offer help and support | • local crisis hot line<br>• family doctor or pediatrician<br>• friends, relatives, neighbors<br>• others in your community |